COLOR YOURSELF INSPIRED

The Bible Promise Book®

Coloring Book

FOR HOPE & HEALING

COLOR YOURSELF INSPIRED

The Bible Promise Book®

Coloring Book

FOR HOPE & HEALING

BARBOUR BOOKS
An Imprint of Barbour Publishing, Inc.

IF THE SON THEREFORE shall make you free, ye shall be free indeed.

(JOHN 8:36)

Casting all your care upon him; for he careth for you.

(1 PETER 5:7)

I AM COME that they might HAVE LIFE, AND THAT they might have it more ABUNDANTLY.

(JOHN 10:10)

He healeth the broken in heart, and bindeth up their wounds.

(PSALM 147:3)

My flesh
and my heart faileth:
but GOD
is the strength
of my heart,
and my portion
for ever.

(PSALM 73:26)

THOU WILT KEEP HIM IN PERFECT PEACE, WHOSE MIND is stayed on thee: BECAUSE HE TRUSTETH IN THEE. (ISAIAH 26:3)

THE LORD preserveth all them THAT LOVE HIM

(PSALM 145:20)

Trust in him at all times...
pour out your heart
before him :
God
is a refuge for us.

(PSALM 62:8)

the LORD UPHOLDETH ALL THAT FALL, AND raiseth up ALL THOSE that be BOWED DOWN.

(PSALM 145:14)

WHEN I FALL,
I SHALL ARISE;
WHEN I SIT
in darkness,
THE LORD
SHALL BE
a light unto me.

(MICAH 7:8)

IF WE ASK any thing according to his will, HE HEARETH US.

(1 JOHN 5:14)

I AM WITH THEE TO SAVE THEE and TO DELIVER THEE saith THE LORD.

(JEREMIAH 15:20)

WITH GOD all things are POSSIBLE.

(MATTHEW 19:26)

Surely goodness and
mercy shall follow me
all the days of my life:
and I will dwell
in the house of the
LORD for ever.

PSALM 23:6

The LORD knoweth the days of the UPRIGHT and their inheritance shall be FOR EVER.

PSALM 37:18

Thanks be to God, which giveth us the victory through our Lord Jesus Christ.

1 CORINTHIANS 15:57

BLESSED ARE THEY THAT MOURN; COMFORTED. FOR THEY SHALL BE

MATTHEW 5:4

Bless the Lord, O my soul,
and forget not all his benefits:

who forgiveth all thine iniquities;
who healeth all thy diseases.

Psalm 103:2-3

UNTO YOU THAT FEAR MY NAME SHALL

THE SUN OF RIGHTEOUSNESS ARISE WITH HEALING IN HIS WINGS.

Malachi 4:2

I will seek that which was lost, and bring again that which was driven away, and will bind up that which was broken, and will strengthen that which was sick.

Ezekiel 34:16

THE PRAYER OF FAITH SHALL SAVE THE SICK, AND THE LORD SHALL RAISE HIM UP.

James 5:15

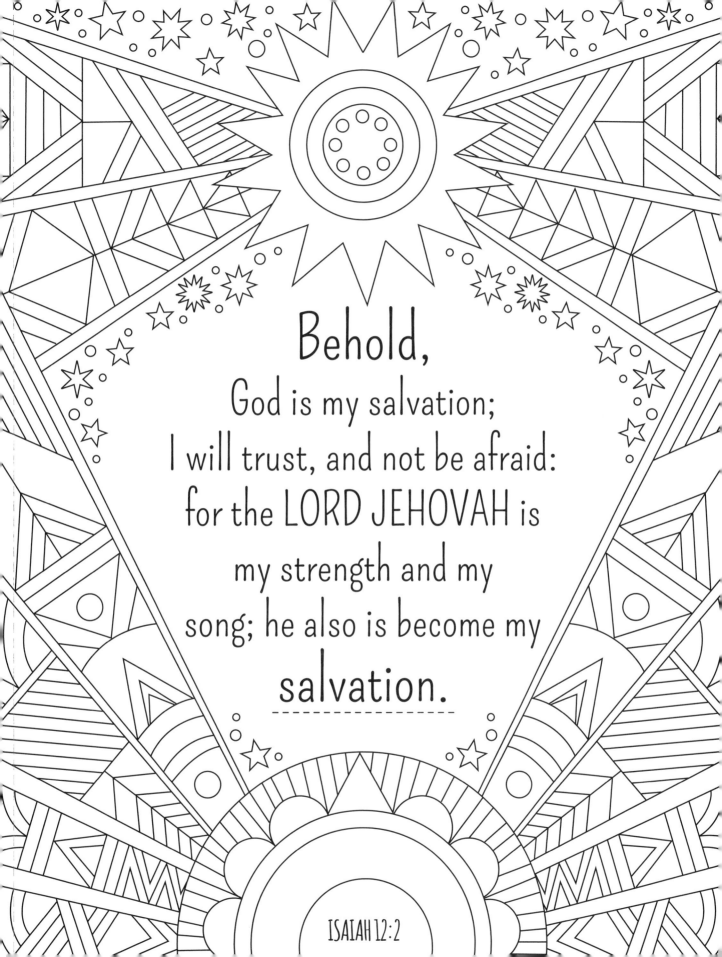

Behold,
God is my salvation;
I will trust, and not be afraid:
for the LORD JEHOVAH is
my strength and my
song; he also is become my
salvation.

ISAIAH 12:2

Therefore if any man be in Christ, he is a new creature: old things are passed away; behold, all things are become new.

2 CORINTHIANS 5:17

Lo, I am with you
ALWAYS,
even unto
the end of the
WORLD.
AMEN.

MATTHEW 28:20

1 JOHN 4:18

In the world ye shall have tribulation: but be of good cheer; I have overcome the WORLD

JOHN 16:33

I will both lay me down in PEACE, & SLEEP: for thou, LORD only makest me dwell in safety.

PSALM 4:8

MY GRACE

is sufficient for thee:

for my

STRENGTH

is made perfect in

weakness.

2 CORINTHIANS 12:9

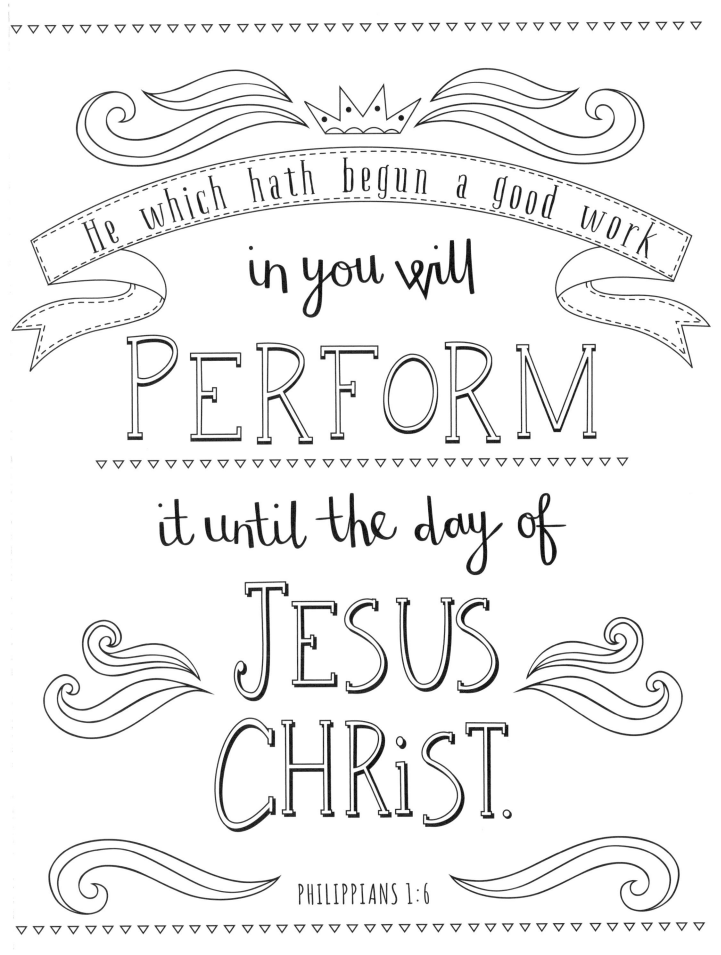

Because he hath inclined his ear unto me, therefore will I call upon him as long as I Live.

PSALM 116:2

But my God shall supply all your need according to his riches in glory by **Christ Jesus.**

PHILIPPIANS 4:19

Now the God
of hope fill you with all

Joy & Peace

In believing, that ye may abound in hope,
through the power of the

Holy
Ghost.

Romans 15:13

COME UNTO ME, ALL YE THAT LABOUR AND ARE HEAVY LADEN, AND I WILL GIVE YOU REST.

matthew 11:28

THE WATER THAT I SHALL GIVE... SHALL BE IN HIM A WELL *of* WATER SPRINGING · UP · INTO EVERLASTING LIFE.

John 4:14

THE Lord THY GOD IN THE MIDST OF THEE IS MIGHTY; HE WILL SAVE, HE WILL REJOICE OVER THEE WITH Joy; HE WILL REST IN HIS LOVE, HE WILL JOY OVER THEE WITH SINGING.

ZEPHANIAH 3:17

BEHOLD,

I MAKE ALL THINGS NEW.

REVELATION 21:5